Presented To:

_____

By:

_____

Date:

_____

•   •   •

Everyday Prayers
for
Everyday Cares

. . .

Honor Books
Tulsa, Oklahoma

INTRODUCTION

If you are reading this book, you must be like the rest of us—anxious to find an outlet for the cares of your everyday life. What better way to do that than through simple, everyday prayers to your loving Heavenly Father! Whether you access them daily or only in times of distress, the prayers in this book have been designed to build you up in your faith and provide an anchor for your soul as you make your way through life's storm-tossed seas.

We have included a scripture from the Bible with each of these meditative prayers. And we have arranged them topically so that you can find just what you need when you need it.

So take a few moments to make these prayers your own. Open your heart and your hands to receive God's glorious promises, and apply them to the circumstances you are facing.

May God bless you as you take time to be with Him.

CONTENTS

When

I Feel Angry . . .

"Be angry, and do not sin": do not let the sun go down on your wrath.

Ephesians 4:26

Father,

You help me overcome my angry thoughts and emotions.

You are so patient with me, and You help me to be patient with others. You don't ask me to deny my anger or pretend it away, but You give me the courage I need to face it honestly—and forgive. You encourage me to seek reconciliation with those who have offended me. Thank You for the peace that comes from doing things Your way.

Amen.

> *He who is slow to wrath has great understanding, But he who is impulsive exalts folly.*
>
> PROVERBS 14:29

FATHER,

You are my Source of patience and understanding.

When life is frustrating and I feel anger building within me, it is so good to know that You are as close as my breath, calming the storm inside my head and giving me the self-control I need to think before I respond with harsh words. You are so faithful to smooth out my ruffled feathers and help me regain my inner peace.

Amen.

Therefore, my beloved brethren, let every man be swift to hear, slow to speak, slow to wrath; for the wrath of man does not produce the righteousness of God.

JAMES 1:19-20

FATHER,

Your love guides me in all my relationships.

Most of the time, it's those I love most who stir up my angry emotions. Thank You for quieting my heart and helping me to see the underlying cause of my anger—whether it be exhaustion, anxiety, or fear. Thank You for reminding me to consider the person I am in conflict with. When You help me in these ways, You enable me to act wisely, measure my words carefully, and preserve rather than destroy my most important relationships.

Amen.

Do not be overcome by evil, but overcome evil with good.

FATHER,

With Your help, I can overcome evil with good.

When I am angry and overwhelmed by hurt, my first response is to lash out, fight back, and get even. But I know that You are pleased when I seek Your peace and trust You to help me focus on unconditional love and forgiveness. Give me a heart big enough to choose good, to bless and not retaliate, and to look for the hidden blessing in the midst of every difficult situation.

Amen.

• • •

When

I FEEL ANXIOUS . . .

"I know the plans I have for you," declares the
LORD, "plans to prosper you and not to harm
you, plans to give you hope and a future."

JEREMIAH 29:11 NIV

FATHER,

I know You have great plans for me.

When I look at my life, I often see chaos, change, and confusion. I become anxious, afraid that my dreams will never come true. But You say that I have a future and a hope, that marvelous plans will one day be revealed in their fullness. Today I choose to rest in that hope and believe that You will help me fulfill every dream You have placed in my heart.

Amen.

We know that all things work together for good to those who love God, to those who are called according to his purpose.

ROMANS 8:28

FATHER,

You always keep Your promises.

I have no reason to be anxious or fearful because You have promised that You will make every circumstance in my life work together for my good. I can trust You. When I look back on my life, I see that You have been there in every situation. You promise me a good future. And in this present moment, You are here with me.

Amen.

•   •   •

When

I NEED ASSURANCE . . .

---

*For it is the God who commanded light to
shine out of darkness, who has shone in our
hearts to give the light of the knowledge of the
glory of God in the face of Jesus Christ.*

---

2 CORINTHIANS 4:6

FATHER,

You shine the light of Your love into my darkness.

Sometimes I feel like a child lost in the dark, but You
come to me in my night and offer reassurance. You light
a candle in my heart, illuminating my darkness with Your
love and grace. You assure me that You will never leave
me nor forsake me—that Your light will be with me,
comforting me through every moment of my life.

Amen.

> *Cast your burden on the LORD, And He shall sustain you; He shall never permit the righteous to be moved.*

PSALM 55:22

FATHER,

You are the One who carries my burdens.

When the road is rocky and I am weary, You come along beside me. You do not condemn my weakness; but instead, You offer me Your strength. In times of doubt, You help me find faith. You are always there when I call. You promise never to forsake or leave me. You are my Strength, my Fortress, and my Rock. I can rest assured in Your love and Your strength.

Amen.

* * *

When

I NEED HELP WITH
MY CHILDREN . . .

All your children shall be taught by the LORD,
And great shall be the peace of your children.

ISAIAH 54:13

FATHER,

You teach me—and my children.

When I feel confused and overwhelmed by my parenting responsibilities, I remember You are here with me, patiently giving me the wisdom and insight I need to shepherd my little flock. You give me a strong arm to lean on when I see my children making poor choices. You promise to go with them where I cannot, to watch over them, and to show them the right path.

Amen.

And he will turn the hearts of the fathers to the children, And the hearts of the children to their fathers.

MALACHI 4:6

FATHER,

You are the great Communicator.

I thank You for the precious children You have given me. I know You will help me encourage them to become all that they are meant to be. As they go through different stages of growth, I will look to You for the right words with which to guide, encourage, strengthen, and instruct them.

Amen.

•　•　•

When

I NEED COMFORT . . .

THE LORD *is my light and my salvation;*
Whom shall I fear? The LORD *is the strength*
of my life; Of whom shall I be afraid?

PSALM 27:1

FATHER,

You provide a safe place for me to ride out the storms of life.

When I am feeling lost and afraid, You comfort me and light up the dark corners of my life. You hold my hand and lead me gently through troubled times. When I am sad or afraid, You cradle me in Your loving arms. I know that You are always with me, and that truth gives me courage and endurance. I praise You, for You are my Comforter and the Lifter of my head.

Amen.

> *GOD is our refuge and strength, A very present help in trouble.*

FATHER,

You are my Refuge in times of trouble.

When I'm in trouble, Lord, I run to You for comfort. I thank You that Your arms are always open to meet me, even when I don't deserve Your love and mercy. You strengthen me and fill me with peace. And You provide a safe haven for me—a place where I can rest, heal, and renew my faith. What a blessing it is to be Your child!

Amen.

> *The LORD is good, A stronghold in the day of trouble; And He knows those who trust in Him.*

NAHUM 1:7

FATHER,

You know me inside and out.

It would be easy for me to sit alone in my sorrow and let grief and self-pity overcome me. But I will not because I know that You are always here with me. You understand what I'm feeling, for You have also experienced sorrow. You see my tears before they even fall from my eyes. You understand my anguish long before I can find words to describe it. And realizing that You know all of this, comforts me and sets me on the path to healing.

Amen.

Casting all your care upon Him, for He cares for you.

1 Peter 5:7

Father,

You always care for me.

When I am feeling alone, buried under a load of problems, You are always there, encouraging me to cast them off and onto You. I will never understand why You care for me, but You do. Your hand is always there to lift me up, and Your arm is always ready to strengthen and support me. No matter what circumstances I encounter in my life, I know that I will not face them alone, because You care for me.

Amen.

•   •   •

When

I NEED HELP AMIDST CONFLICT . . .

Owe no one anything except to love one another, for he who loves another has fulfilled the law.

ROMANS 13:8

FATHER,

You are my safe Harbor in storm-tossed seas.

When I encounter conflict in my life, I always run to You. You know all the details of every situation, and You know the heart of each person involved. I ask now that You have Your way in the conflict I am now facing. Help me to keep my heart open to those things that bring peace and reconciliation. I thank You for giving us the answers we need to resolve our differences and walk together in love.

Amen.

> *Hot tempers start fights; a calm, cool spirit keeps the peace.*

PROVERBS 15:18 THE MESSAGE

FATHER,

You protect and guide me in times of conflict.

When I am in conflict with others, I know You are there to help me rise above the emotions of hurt and anger. You place Your hand upon my mouth until I have repented of my own willfulness and faced my own failings. You pour Your love and forgiveness into my heart and give me the strength to find a pathway to peace. Some people serve gods of retribution, but I serve a God of reconciliation.

Amen.

•   •   •

When

I AM CONFUSED . . .

"I am the good shepherd."

JOHN 10:11

FATHER,

You shepherd my soul.

You are the good Shepherd who seeks the lost sheep. Though I sometimes stray from Your flock, You always come after me and bring me back to the fold. When I am confused and wander from Your will, You call me back lovingly and save me from my own foolishness. You illuminate my path with understanding. And You always lead me safely home.

Amen.

"You shall know the truth, and the truth shall make you free."

JOHN 8:32

FATHER,

You bring clarity to my thoughts.

When I feel confused and anxious, I know that I can come to You and You will settle my mind until I can hear Your voice clearly again. And as soon as I am able to listen, you will speak to me, replacing my uncertainty with Your wisdom. You shine Your light of truth on the situations that baffle me and set me free to make good choices for my life. You strengthen my mind and keep me pointed in the right direction.

Amen.

•　　•　　•

When

I LONG FOR CONTENTMENT . . .

The work of righteousness will be peace, And the effect of righteousness, quietness and assurance forever.

ISAIAH 32:17

FATHER,

You are my Righteousness and my Peace.

When I am feeling dissatisfied with my life, You are my Source of peace and contentment. When I become restless and feel myself striving to own more, accomplish more, and be more; You are there to settle my restless heart and keep me walking on a straight path. You provide a place of rest and contentment for me that I cannot provide for myself.

Amen.

The LORD is my shepherd; I shall not want.

PSALM 23:1

FATHER,

You fill my heart to overflowing.

When my mind is filled with thoughts of what I do not have, I look to You to remind me of all the things You have so graciously placed in my life. I speak them out, enumerating my blessings, so that You and I can celebrate them together. And I lift my voice to praise You for Your abundant love that fills me up until I spill over with joy and delight.

Amen.

> *"Consider the lilies of the field, how they grow."*

MATTHEW 6:28

FATHER,

You make me more than I am.

When I feel my self-worth slipping and long to be as talented and capable as others, You remind me that I am Your creation, fearfully and wonderfully made. There is no need for me to prove myself by doing what others do. You only ask that I do what You have called and equipped me to do. Then you fill my heart with love, acceptance, and peace.

Amen.

Better is a dry morsel with quietness, Than a house full of feasting with strife.

PROVERBS 17:1

FATHER,

You are the Fulfillment of all my longings.

When I am tempted to envy others, You always remind me to keep my eyes on You. You urge me to look to You for the satisfaction and fulfillment my soul desires. You help me to understand that I could have a huge bounty of the world's riches and still be consumed with feelings of emptiness and longing because money cannot buy love, joy, and peace. Only You can bring those things to my life.

Amen.

•　　•　　•

When

I Need Courage . . .

God has not given us a spirit of fear, but of power and of love and of a sound mind.

2 Timothy 1:7

Father,

You are the One who fills me with courage.

How greatly I depend upon Your promise to walk with me through every situation I encounter in my life! You instill in me the courage I need to do all that You ask me to do. You keep my mind clear and focused, free of panic and anxiety. You constantly remind me that I have nothing to fear as long as I have You at my side. You are my strong Tower and ready Defense.

Amen.

A thousand may fall at your side, And ten thousand at your right hand; But it shall not come near you.

PSALM 91:7

FATHER,

You are the One who strengthens me for every battle.

Today, I am faced with difficult choices, and battles are raging around me that threaten to overwhelm my soul. It's so good to know that You are right by my side, providing the strength and courage I need to move forward with peace and confidence. I will depend upon Your steadying arm and Your faithful promises to see me through to victory.

Amen.

You are my hiding place; You shall preserve me from trouble; You shall surround me with songs of deliverance.

FATHER,

You surround me with songs of deliverance.

When I am frightened by the chaos, noise, and storms in my life, You bring songs of deliverance to soothe my soul. Sometimes You speak with the soft whisper of the wind, telling me that Your Spirit is working on my behalf. Other times Your voice sounds like the quiet murmuring of a brook, reminding me that You can part the seas and calm the storms. Your songs of deliverance give me the courage I need to carry on.

Amen.

> *The LORD will be your confidence, And will keep your foot from being caught.*

PROVERBS 3:26

FATHER,

You are my Source of confidence.

Sometimes I am clumsy with fear. I stumble and stammer, whimpering like a child who has fallen down and can't find the courage to stand up again. But You comfort me like a loving parent, encouraging me to get up and take the next step on my journey of faith. Because You strengthen me with Your loving smile, I have the courage to stand up and move forward on the path You have set before me.

Amen.

•   •   •

When

I FEAR DEATH . . .

> *For we know that if our earthly house, this tent, is destroyed, we have a building from God, a house not made with hands, eternal in the heavens.*

2 CORINTHIANS 5:1

FATHER,

You promise me life eternal.

When the fear of death pushes in around me, I remember that You have conquered death and destroyed its power in my life. Though I may suffer the loss of my mortal life, You have promised me that eternal life is waiting beyond the earthly grave. In Heaven I will enjoy an everlasting life, devoid of sorrow, and I will walk in Your presence forever along with family and friends. Thank You for the promise of this eternal life that was purchased for me by Your own precious Son.

Amen.

*Our God is the God of salvation; And to
GOD the Lord belong escapes from death.*

PSALM 68:20

FATHER,

You are the God who saves me.

You give, not only the breath of life in my earthly body, but also the breath of eternal life. Though I come to You with nothing but unworthiness, You assure me that I am being pardoned and found acceptable, not on my own merit, but because of Your enduring mercy and kindness. I take joy in this great provision You have made for me and in its power to free me from the fear of death.

Amen.

The body is sown in corruption, it is raised in incorruption. It is sown in dishonor, it is raised in glory. It is sown in weakness, it is raised in power.

1 CORINTHIANS 15:42-43

FATHER,

You promise to raise us to immortal life.

When I suffer the loss of those who are precious to me, I will remember that You liken our lives here on earth to seeds. When our earthly lives are over and our bodies are buried in the ground, we are like seeds being planted. What happens next can never be fully comprehended by us. Just as a beautiful flower springs up from a seed buried in the earth, we, too, shall burst forth into eternal life. What a glorious promise!

Amen.

> *Jesus said to her, "I am the resurrection and the life. He who believes in Me, though he may die, he shall live."*

JOHN 11:25

FATHER,

You sent Your Son to bring us life.

I have read in the Bible that You raised a little girl, a widow's son, and Your friend Lazarus from the dead. Even more amazing, You yourself rose from the grave three days after Your crucifixion. Then You told Your disciples that You were going on ahead to prepare a place in Heaven for all those who put their trust in You. I am trusting in Your plan, and I thank You that I need not fear even the mystery of death.

Amen.

•   •   •

When

I FEEL DEPRESSED . . .

Being confident of this very thing, that He who has begun a good work in you will complete it until the day of Jesus Christ.

PHILIPPIANS 1:6

FATHER,

You never give up on me.

When the dark cloud of discouragement covers my soul, You are there to assure me that my life has meaning. When I am depressed, You walk with me through the shadows. You are performing a good work in my life. I ask that You will work through my discouragement to teach me. Help me to become a more compassionate, humble, and loving person—complete in You.

Amen.

Let us not grow weary while doing good, for in due season we shall reap if we do not lose heart.

GALATIANS 6:9

FATHER,

You give me strength to go on.

When I am struggling with my dark moods, You are always there to soothe and comfort me. You remind me that one day I will see the sunshine again if I take hold of You and Your glorious promises. You assure me that You will hold my hand through any difficulty I may encounter. I thank You that good seed grows, even when my spirit feels dark, and that good work will come to fruition.

Amen.

You will light my lamp; The LORD my God will enlighten my darkness.

PSALM 18:28

FATHER,

You light up my darkness.

On gloomy days, You provide a gentle, healing light to illuminate the darkness. This light is subtle and soothing. Just as one small candle can light a dark room, one small touch from You can brighten my dark mood. I choose one of the many promises You have given to me and cling to that promise. I give thanks that the light of Your love shines through, bringing hope and healing.

Amen.

> *As a father pities his children, So the LORD*
> *pities those who fear Him. For He knows our*
> *frame; He remembers that we are dust.*

PSALMS 103:13-14

FATHER,

You show me Your tender love.

Sometimes depression comes because I am tired. I have worn myself out with worry and have allowed anxiety to pull me down into a deep dark hole. Instead of resting in the peace You have promised, I have let my fears and worries rule me. I now choose to take time to rest, to eat properly, to exercise, and to sleep. I will take care of my body's needs and rest in Your love.

Amen.

*   *   *

When

I STRUGGLE WITH DISAPPOINTMENT . . .

Why are you cast down, O my soul? And why are you disquieted within me? Hope in God, for I shall yet praise Him For the help of His countenance.

PSALM 42:5

FATHER,

You are my Hope when life lets me down.

Disappointment hurts. My heart aches when it seems as though my dreams will never be fulfilled. But then I remember You. I meditate on the promises You have kept throughout my life. I acknowledge how trustworthy You are. Though people let me down and situations have disappointing results, You are faithful to me. I choose to trust in You in the midst of discouragement, believing that You are always looking out for me.

Amen.

A man's heart plans his way, But the LORD directs his steps.

PROVERBS 16:9

FATHER,

I trust that You work all things together for my good.

I have plans, hopes, and dreams. Sometimes things go my way; but there are also disappointments—obstacles and failures that discourage me. In these tough times, I choose to take my eyes off my troubles and look, instead, to You for guidance. I know You will help me find the hidden blessings in my circumstances. You will guide my steps. With Your help, I will continue to make positive choices and keep hope alive in my heart.

Amen.

• • •

When

I NEED DISCIPLINE . . .

Yet in all these things we are more than conquerors through Him who loved us.

ROMANS 8:37

FATHER,

You help me live victoriously.

You give me the strength and tenacity to continue in times of difficulty and discouragement. Through simple daily practice, I discipline my heart to follow Your ways and make choices for the highest good. I take baby steps instead of expecting giant leaps of faith. You give me the energy to do what needs to be done and the wisdom to know how to pace myself. Your yoke is easy, and Your burden is light.

Amen.

> *Therefore do not cast away your confidence, which has great reward. For you have need of endurance, so that after you have done the will of God, you may receive the promise.*

HEBREWS 10:35-36

FATHER,

You encourage and strengthen me.

You teach me how to be balanced and healthy in my approach to life: resting and playing in a natural rhythm with work. You remind me that "all work and no play" is as unhealthy as "no work and all play." You help me find a happy medium—a safe way to accomplish goals and grow as a person. Thank You for showing me that I need discipline in *all* areas of my life.

Amen.

•   •   •

When

I Am Discouraged . . .

I waited patiently for the LORD; And He inclined to me, And heard my cry.

PSALM 40:1

FATHER,

You believe in me.

You see the whole picture, while I only see what is here before me. When I am so discouraged that I feel like I can't even lift my head, You speak to me. You give me an eternal perspective on this temporary situation. You show me that Your plans are much greater for me than I can imagine. Because You believe in me, I can find the courage to believe in myself and in the dreams You have placed in my heart.

Amen.

> *Though he fall, he shall not be utterly cast down;*
> *For the LORD upholds him with His hand.*

PSALM 37:24

FATHER,

You are my Glory and the Lifter of my head.

When life seems to fall apart around me, I know I must look to You. You will bring order out of chaos, light out of darkness, and courage in the midst of discouragement. Though my heart is heavy, You take the weight of my problems and lighten my load. You help me persevere, guiding me across my desert to a promised land, just as you did with the children of Israel.

Amen.

•   •   •

When

I AM DOUBTFUL . . .

So we may boldly say: "The LORD is my helper; I will not fear. What can man do to me?"

HEBREWS 13:6

FATHER,

You give me boldness in times of doubt.

Sometimes doubt makes me feel as if I'm in a wrestling match. I try to believe Your promises and to have faith, but then my doubts and fears fight with my faith, telling me that I'm a failure and that I can never succeed. You show me that doubt is natural—without it our faith would have no foundation. No matter what my situation, You help me take the next step in my journey of faith.

Amen.

Then they cried out to the LORD in their trouble,
And He delivered them out of their distresses.

PSALM 107:6

FATHER,

You deliver me from all my fears.

Whether or not I feel Your presence, I know that You are with me. You do not despise me for doubting. Instead, You help me to find faith in the midst of my fear. You encourage me to look for solutions to difficult problems and to trust You in spite of the circumstances that surround me. When I make a conscious choice to trust, clarity and peace fill my heart. I am enriched and encouraged by Your faithfulness.

Amen.

•   •   •

When

I NEED ENCOURAGEMENT . . .

He shall be like a tree Planted by the rivers of water, That brings forth its fruit in its season.

PSALM 1:3

FATHER,

You are my River of living water.

Like a tree planted by deep streams, I am rooted in Your goodness and love. I come to You and find rivers of living water, springs of encouragement, and strength and nourishment for my weary heart. Because I trust in You, I can continue to grow in grace, even during trying times. Thank You for lifting me up and filling my heart with gladness.

Amen.

Be of good courage, And He shall strengthen your heart, All you who hope in the LORD.

PSALM 31:24

FATHER,

You strengthen my heart.

At times, it feels as if everybody is telling me what I'm doing wrong or why I can't become the person I yearn to be. But I know that You have a plan and purpose for me, and You are working in my life to carry out Your plan. When I feel as if the world misunderstands me or is against me, I look to You for strength. Help me find courage as I hope in You.

Amen.

Immediately Jesus spoke to them, saying, "Be of good cheer! It is I; do not be afraid."

MATTHEW 14:27

FATHER,

You send me help at just the right time.

I've read in the Bible about the disciples, marooned in a boat in the middle of a storm-tossed lake. They must have felt helpless. Then Jesus came to them, walking on the water, and He calmed the storm. Sometimes, when I am in the middle of a storm, I think my small boat will capsize and all will be lost. But You always send me help. Thank You for miracles of encouragement that arrive in unexpected times and places.

Amen.

Oh, taste and see that the LORD is good;
Blessed is the man who trusts in Him!

PSALM 34:8

FATHER,

You are my Source.

When I need encouragement, I look around and count my blessings, for I know that I always have reason to give thanks for Your goodness in my life. I thank You for family, friends, food, and shelter. I thank You for the beauty that surrounds me in the world. I thank You for sunlight, rain, and green growing things. I take time to stop and smell the roses—and I am encouraged by Your constant goodness.

Amen.

*   *   *

When

I NEED ENDURANCE . . .

---

*Then He spoke a parable to them, that men
always ought to pray and not lose heart.*

LUKE 18:1

FATHER,

You hear my prayers.

You tell me to pray without ceasing. Sometimes my prayers seem to reach no higher than the ceiling. But even when I feel like quitting, I know You are listening. So I keep praying, trusting, and believing—even when I feel tired and depleted. You give me the courage to persist until I see my prayers answered.

Amen.

Perseverance must finish its work so that you may be mature and complete, not lacking anything.

JAMES 1:4 NIV

FATHER,

You help me to persevere.

Some journeys seem endless. I want to ask, "Haven't I learned enough, Lord?" Yet I know that You are helping me, not only in the turbulent times, but also in the monotonous ones when I am simply waiting. Sometimes, those are the most difficult times because I want everything to be wrapped up and resolved. I trust that You will help me to become mature and complete as I focus not on the situation, but on You.

Amen.

* * *

When

I FEEL LIKE A FAILURE . . .

---

*I will praise You, for I am fearfully and won-
derfully made.*

PSALM 139:14

FATHER,

You are my Maker—and You make no mistakes.

There are days when I just can't measure up to expectations—my own or anyone else's. I feel like a failure in
the sight of the world. But You tell me that I am fearfully
and wonderfully made, created for good works in this
place and this time. The Scriptures are full of stories of
"failures" that You transformed into men and women of
faith and success. I choose to believe that my failures are
stepping stones to success in Your Kingdom.

Amen.

> *God has chosen the foolish things of the world to put to shame the wise, and God has chosen the weak things of the world to put to shame the things which are mighty.*

1 CORINTHIANS 1:27

FATHER,

You chose me.

I may feel like a failure in the sight of the world, but I am not a failure in Your eyes. You created me, You called me, and You chose me. You work in mysterious ways—ways that are different from what our mortal minds can fathom. You work by Your system, in Your time. Your strength glorifies and transforms my weakness.

Amen.

*   *   *

When

I NEED FAITH . . .

---

*Whatever is born of God overcomes the world.
And this is the victory that has overcome the
world—our faith.*

---

1 JOHN 5:4

FATHER,

You give me victory through faith.

Faith is indeed a gift. But it does not come in a package of power, strength, and self-confidence. Sometimes this gift of faith is as subtle as a wisp of a breeze—barely detectable, but present and effective nonetheless. So today, I ask for the measure of Your great gift that I need to impact this world for Your Kingdom. Today, I ask for faith and thank You for giving it to me generously.

Amen.

So then faith comes by hearing, and hearing by the word of God.

ROMANS 10:17

FATHER,

Your Word generates faith in my heart.

I feed my faith by spending time in Your Word. I meditate on Your promises. I read the stories of those who encountered You and found You to be true and just. My faith grows because I nurture it with Scripture and prayer. You have given me a simple way to find faith: I open my heart and listen to You, the Source and Object of my faith.

Amen.

We walk by faith, not by sight.

2 CORINTHIANS 5:7

FATHER,

You lead me gently and faithfully.

Right now my path is not certain. But I know that if I put my trust in You, I will be guided one small step at a time. Like walking on a trail through fog, I can only see a short way ahead. So I take the next step in faith. Each simple step leads to the one after. You gently walk beside me, leading me through the heavy clouds of doubt and uncertainty into the clear light of day.

Amen.

Now faith is the substance of things hoped for,
the evidence of things not seen.

HEBREWS 11:1

FATHER,

You are the Author and Finisher of my faith.

You are pleased with each little baby step I take. You do not condemn me because I have a faith that seems so small. Instead, You take delight in my choice to trust in You, and You help me in my weakness. One small step of faith becomes a giant leap into things hoped for, because it is Your strength that carries me and leads me home. I give thanks that You are gently leading me each day.

Amen.

The LORD God is a sun and shield; The LORD will give grace and glory; No good thing will He withhold From those who walk uprightly.

PSALM 84:11

FATHER,

You are my Shield and Protector.

I do not need to be afraid. Though fiery darts come at me, You protect me from their burning sting. I can walk confidently through all the battles of life, for You are my powerful ally. Nothing can harm me as long as I trust in You. I will strive to walk uprightly, that I may receive grace and glory from You.

Amen.

• • •

When

I FEEL FEARFUL . . .

Yea, though I walk through the valley of the shadow of death, I will fear no evil; For You are with me.

PSALM 23:4

FATHER,

You are faithful and true.

Sometimes I am amazed at my own lack of faith. You have always kept Your promises, taken care of me, and walked with me through the shadows of life. Yet here I am again, feeling as if You are going to let me down at any moment. How can I feel this way when I know better? As I remember Your goodness to me in the past, I choose to trust that You will provide for me here and now.

Amen.

You did not receive the spirit of bondage again to fear.

ROMANS 8:15

FATHER,

You free me from my fears.

Fear can be a prison. When I am afraid, I am rendered helpless. I try to second guess where trouble will come from next. Instead of imagining creative solutions to my problems, I look for all the ways things can go wrong. I hand these fears over to You. When I learn to trust You, I begin to look for the best instead of expecting the worst. You deliver me from my fears and unlock my prison door.

Amen.

When you pass through the waters, I will be with you.

Isaiah 43:2

FATHER,

You are with me at all times.

When I am tempted to be afraid, I rest in Your presence and let You calm the stormy emotional seas that threaten to overwhelm me. There is no situation so perilous that You cannot break through and reach me. As I take time to quiet my fears, I can hear Your still, small voice speaking to me, assuring me that You will always be by my side. Your presence will carry me through the deep and perilous seas to a safe harbor.

Amen.

•   •   •

When

I NEED HELP WITH
MY FINANCES . . .

"Give us this day our daily bread."

MATTHEW 6:11

FATHER,

You provide for each day's needs.

When I worry about the future, You tell me to ask for enough for today. You take care of me one day at a time. Just as the Israelites found enough manna for the day's needs, so I find enough money for today's requirements. I thank You that I have food to eat, money to pay the bills, health to do my work, and faith to trust You with tomorrow.

Amen.

God is able to make all grace abound toward you, that you, always having all sufficiency in all things, may have an abundance for every good work.

2 CORINTHIANS 9:8

FATHER,

You are the God of abundance.

You promise that I will always have enough—and more than enough. Though I may not have worldly riches, I have Heavenly riches that fill my life abundantly. You give me good gifts and empower me to do good work. You provide the resources I need to do Your will. If money is necessary for the work You call me to, then money will come to me. I anticipate Your provision for every need.

Amen.

He satisfies the longing soul, And fills the hungry soul with goodness.

FATHER,

You satisfy me with goodness.

I count my blessings and find myself rich in You. When I take the time to be thankful for what I already have, I discover that I have more than enough. You give me prudence and wisdom to handle my finances honorably. You give me the ability to make money, and You help me to spend it wisely. Though my sinful nature always wants more, my heart is satisfied with what I already have. Your goodness is more than enough.

Amen.

Worthy is the Lamb who was slain To receive power and riches and wisdom.

REVELATION 5:12

FATHER,

You are worthy of my praise.

Thank You for the gifts and resources You have given me. I honor You by dedicating myself to Your service. Like the little boy who gave Jesus his lunch of loaves and fishes, I know that You will bless and multiply the gifts I give to You. And through them, You will feed a hungry world as you have fed my hungry soul. I sow abundantly and reap richly. I praise You for Your faithfulness.

Amen.

* * *

When

I NEED TO FORGIVE . . .

"Forgive us our debts, As we forgive our debtors."

MATTHEW 6:12

FATHER,

You teach me forgiveness.

It's so easy to hold grudges. I often find myself adding up all the things that others have done wrong, forgetting all the things I have left undone. But You teach me that forgiveness is not an option, but rather a Kingdom necessity. And when I forgive those who have trespassed against me, I realize that I have opened the doors of my heart to forgive myself. No longer weighing and measuring who did what to whom, I love others in freedom and joy.

Amen.

> *"Love your enemies, do good, and lend, hoping for nothing in return; and your reward will be great, and you will be sons of the Most High. For He is kind to the unthankful and evil."*

LUKE 6:35

FATHER,

You are kind to all of us.

When I feel that I have been sinned against, I need only to look into my own heart to see that I struggle with the same sins. Father, I thank You that You are generous and forgiving to us all. You forgive those who trespass against me. But even more, you forgive me when I am at my worst. Because of Your mercy, I choose to be merciful too.

Amen.

Though your sins are like scarlet, They shall be as white as snow.

ISAIAH 1:18

FATHER,

You forgive me.

My heart is heavy because of what I have done—and because of what I have left undone. I have not loved others the way You love me. I have judged and belittled them. I have not done the things I wanted to do. I have done what I now wish I could undo. Yet when I come to You, I am not turned away. Instead, You forgive me, cleanse me, and give me mercy so I can begin anew.

Amen.

• • •

When

I NEED FORGIVENESS . . .

*For the Scripture says, "Whoever believes in
Him will not be put to shame."*

ROMANS 10:11

FATHER,

You lift me up.

When I feel ashamed, You tell me that Your love covers
all my shame. When I feel like a failure, You tell me that
You see a precious and beloved child. Right now I come
to You, asking forgiveness. And I thank You that You not
only forgive me, but also remove my shame and sadness.
You make my heart sing with renewed joy because Your
love lifts me up from the depths into Your cleansing light.

Amen.

> *"Therefore I say to you, her sins, which are many, are forgiven, for she loved much."*

LUKE 7:47

FATHER,

You help me to accept forgiveness and to love others.

You are generous with Your children. You forgive us so we can learn to love one another, give grace to one another, and see You in each other. To love is to understand, and to understand is to forgive. I have compassion on others and, therefore, learn more about the compassion You have for me. Every time I stumble, it is a new opportunity to learn sweet lessons of forgiveness and grace.

Amen.

> *BLESSED is he whose transgression is forgiven,*
> *Whose sin is covered.*

PSALM 32:1

FATHER,

Your grace is a gift that cannot be earned.

You are not stingy with grace. You give forgiveness and mercy freely. Though I may condemn myself, You do not condemn me. When I expect curses, You bless me. You forgive us all so that we may be one family in You. Because of Your mercy and grace, I am blessed beyond measure. I am lifted up and able to stand for what is right.

Amen.

.   .   .

When

I Need a Friend . . .

"By this all will know that you are My disciples, if you have love for one another."

John 13:35

Father,

You send me people to love.

You are my Friend. But You also bring me friends. You bring people into my life who love and honor You by loving and honoring each other. You have placed the solitary in a spiritual family. We may be from different backgrounds and have different interests, but we are all one in You. Thank You for those You have placed in my life. Help me love them as You love me.

Amen.

We took sweet counsel together, And walked to the house of God in the throng.

PSALM 55:14

FATHER,

I find fellowship when I worship You.

Thank You for the friends You have given me, especially those who share my faith in You. We travel through life together, offering our gifts, not only to You, but also to each other. Our hearts are knit together by our love for You. You empower us to love and show us how to serve one another. I feel such a special bond with those who love You as I do. I thank You for placing these friends in my life.

Amen.

A friend loves at all times, And a brother is born for adversity.

PROVERBS 17:17

FATHER,

You give me the gift of friendship.

I thank You for giving me friends who are unique and different from each other and from me. It causes us to grow in character as we learn to support one another in spite of our differences. How wise and wonderful You are! I appreciate the way You have extended Your love to me through the friends You have placed in my life.

Amen.

> *He Himself has said, "I will never leave you nor forsake you."*

HEBREWS 13:5

FATHER,

You are a trustworthy Friend.

When I am alone, I have a Friend in You. You are my best Friend, the One who will never leave me nor forsake me. Human beings sometimes disappoint me, and I often fail them as well. But even though I am separated from friends and loved ones by physical or emotional distance, You are always near. You are a Friend to the friendless and the God who is always with me.

Amen.

•   •   •

When

I Am Frustrated . . .

For this is the will of God, that by doing good you may put to silence the ignorance of foolish men.

---

1 Peter 2:15

FATHER,

You keep me on a straight path.

In this world, it is easy to go astray. Frustration tempts me to leave the right paths and try to find shortcuts to fulfill my dreams. Many people say that the way to get ahead is to push past everyone else and that climbing the ladder of success means stepping on others. But You help me to be patient, gentle, and good. You help me harness my frustration and use its energy to walk down a good path.

Amen.

> *Therefore do not let sin reign in your mortal body, that you should obey it in its lusts.*

ROMANS 6:12

FATHER,

You help me live according to Your principles.

Our society equates lust with sex. But there is also a lust for power—the urge to get while the getting is good, before someone else grabs our share. You show me that patient love is the answer to the frustrations of our hurry-up-and-get-it society. You remind me that the Kingdom of God is not meat or drink, but righteousness, peace, and joy. Give me the strength to live according to Your Spirit.

Amen.

Do not hasten in your spirit to be angry, For anger rests in the bosom of fools.

ECCLESIASTES 7:9

FATHER,

You quiet my spirit.

When someone cuts in front of me in traffic, the line at the bank is long, I miss a deadline, or someone takes advantage of me; You are there to remind me that I have a choice to make. Either I can respond with anger, or I can choose to trust in You. In these difficult times, I choose to replace the choppy waves of frustration with the still waters of Your peace. You still my spirit like a mother quiets her child.

Amen.

A fool's wrath is known at once, But a prudent man covers shame.

FATHER,

You give me wisdom and patience.

I come to You once more, sorry for something I said in frustration. I didn't mean to lash out at that other person. I didn't mean to make the situation worse. I ask for Your forgiveness. I also ask that You would help me guard my tongue and quiet my troubled spirit. I thank You that You freely forgive, offering me wisdom, peace, and patience for frustrating days. Next time I will hold my peace and trust You.

Amen.

•   •   •

Everyday Prayers for Everyday Cares • 83

When

I AM SEARCHING FOR FULFILLMENT . . .

Delight yourself also in the LORD, And He shall give you the desires of your heart.

PSALM 37:4

FATHER,

You are my heart's Desire.

I love you, Father. I come to You, knowing that I will find peace and rest in Your presence. I thank You that You are even now leading me to my heart's desire. You not only give me what my heart wants most, but You also teach my heart to want what is best for me. Your love fulfills my deepest desire, and every other earthly fulfillment is a gift from You.

Amen.

Then you shall delight yourself in the LORD;
And I will cause you to ride on the high hills
of the earth.

ISAIAH 58:14

FATHER,

You are my Delight.

I do not have to look far and wide for fulfillment. You are my Fulfillment. Into my heart, You have placed sweet dreams and a yearning for something that I can't even put into words. I thank You that You offer gentle hints of Heavenly fulfillment to come in the earthly joys of each day. I rest in the knowledge that my dreams and yearning find fulfillment in Your time.

Amen.

> *"Ask, and it will be given to you; seek, and you will find; knock, and it will be opened to you."*

MATTHEW 7:7

FATHER,

You give me the best gifts.

You tell me to ask, seek, and knock. I seek the best gifts by seeking You. I will be persistent in pursuing Your best for me, knowing that You will open only the right doors. I step out in faith, obedient to Your Word, and I trust that You will bring me to a place of fulfillment and joy. You are a generous God who gives His children good gifts. My heart rejoices in Your goodness.

Amen.

> *For I consider that the sufferings of this present time are not worthy to be compared with the glory which shall be revealed in us.*
>
> ROMANS 8:18

FATHER,

You are my eternal Reward.

I thank You for the beautiful gifts of this earthly life. I thank You for all my answered prayers and fulfilled dreams. But I also know that my deepest fulfillment will never be found on this side of the grave. You promise me that no matter what suffering I experience, no matter what goals I accomplish, Your eternal gifts are far greater. I will find complete fulfillment only with You in eternity. *Amen.*

• • •

When

I Am Grieving . . .

This is my comfort in my affliction, For Your word has given me life.

PSALM 119:50

FATHER,

Your Word is my comfort.

In times of sadness, You give me solace. I treasure Your promises and trust You in the midst of my sorrow. I know that I do not grieve without hope. You are my Hope. You wrap me in Your love. You comfort me with the peace that passes understanding. I hold onto precious promises by faith and find the heart of my life in You.

Amen.

"Blessed are those who mourn, For they shall be comforted."

MATTHEW 5:4

FATHER,

You bless me even as I mourn.

To everything there is a season appointed under Heaven. This is a time of sorrow for me, but I am not alone in my grief. You are with me, and You give me peace and strength to bear my grief. I praise You for Your tender compassion. And I trust You to comfort me during this time of sorrow by continuing to remind me that I will smile again one day soon.

Amen.

As a mother comforts her child, so will I comfort you.

ISAIAH 66:13 NIV

FATHER,

You show tenderness and mercy.

I am Your child, and I know You love me with a tenderness that is even greater than that of an earthly parent. When I am grieving from a loss or disappointment, You are saddened by my hurt. But You also see past it to a brighter day to come. Your tender care brings me comfort as You work to heal me and restore my joy. Thank You, my Father, for Your loving care.

Amen.

• • •

When

I NEED GUIDANCE . . .

---

*Your ears shall hear a word behind you, saying,
"This is the way, walk in it," Whenever you
turn to the right hand Or whenever you turn
to the left.*

ISAIAH 30:21

FATHER,

You promise to guide me.

I often wonder which way to go. But when I'm uncertain, I listen for Your still, small voice. Sometimes Your voice will come as intuition. Sometimes it will be a wise word from a friend. Sometimes circumstances will unfold, and my path will become clear. No matter which way guidance comes, it is You who leads me in the right path for my life.

Amen.

> *The steps of a good man are ordered by the*
> *LORD, And He delights in his way.*

PSALM 37:23

FATHER,

You delight in my choices.

You have given me the gift of free choice. Sometimes the gift seems like a burden, for the responsibility to make the right choices is great. But the gift of a free will offers a wonderful opportunity for me to choose Your ways. When I make choices according to Your will, I know that they are pleasing to You. Thank You for trusting me to do what is right.

Amen.

> *"Therefore do not worry about tomorrow, for tomorrow will worry about its own things. Sufficient for the day is its own trouble."*

MATTHEW 6:34

FATHER,

You guide me day by day.

I know what I need to do today. Though I have many questions and worries about tomorrow, I choose to trust You here and now, right this minute. You will guide me step by step, even when I cannot see the road in front of me. I trust Your gentle guidance and will not worry about tomorrow's troubles. Your mercies are new every morning.

Amen.

> *It shall come to pass That before they call, I will answer; And while they are still speaking, I will hear.*

FATHER,

You anticipate my needs.

You know what I need even before I know what I want. You are there, preparing the way. All I need to do is walk faithfully in the light You give me today. I often believe I know what's ahead, only to be wrong. You guide me into joys I could not have imagined and save me from troubles I could not have foreseen. You answer before I even call.

Amen.

*   *   *

When

I AM SEARCHING FOR HAPPINESS . . .

They are abundantly satisfied with the full-ness of Your house, And You give them drink from the river of Your pleasures.

PSALM 36:8

FATHER,

You teach me to find happiness in the small things.

You teach me to count my blessings, and as I do, I realize that I am happy. A good meal, a safe place to sleep, the laughter of friends, the quiet joys of my daily routine—all are ways You make happiness available to me. Not how much I have, but what I appreciate brings joy to my heart. As I consciously focus on the everyday blessings in my life, I am overwhelmed by Your goodness to me.

Amen.

My spirit has rejoiced in God my Savior.

LUKE 1:47

FATHER,

I rejoice in You.

As Mary said in the Bible, I, too, rejoice in God my Savior. So often, I look to other things for fulfillment and happiness when You are the true Source of real joy. You have looked on me with mercy and have saved me through Your gifts of love and grace. Your works are marvelous. Even when my circumstances are unhappy or difficult, I find joy in trusting and praising You.

Amen.

> *You crown the year with Your goodness, And*
> *Your paths drip with abundance.*

PSALM 65:11

FATHER,

You crown my life with abundance.

I do not look for the frenetic "happiness" that the world promises. Flashy clothes, fast cars, power, and fame will all fade away. Instead I walk in Your paths, knowing that You will lead me to abundant joy and lasting peace. I enjoy seasons of plenty in my life, and I wait patiently in seasons of limitation. I know that You are working all things together for my good––and You will provide everything I need.

Amen.

> *"If you then, being evil, know how to give good gifts to your children, how much more will your Father who is in heaven give good things to those who ask Him!"*

MATTHEW 7:11

FATHER,

You give good things to Your children.

If a child asks for bread, a good parent will not give that child a stone. You are better than even the best earthly parent. You love to give good things to me when I ask. But You are also wise and will not give me everything I crave. You give good gifts to me only when You know I am ready for them. Because You know me so well, I am confident that Your gifts will make me truly happy.

Amen.

•   •   •

When

I NEED HEALING . . .

The LORD will strengthen him on his bed of illness; You will sustain him on his sickbed.

PSALM 41:3

FATHER,

I find strength in You.

My spirit is willing to receive Your healing, but my flesh is weak. As I cope with illness, I learn to find my strength in You. You fill me with Your love and sustain me in times of pain and stress. You are also faithful to send others to help me when I am too weak to help myself. You strengthen my faith and help me work with my body to bring it the healing it needs.

Amen.

Behold, I will bring it health and healing; I will heal them and reveal to them the abundance of peace and truth.

JEREMIAH 33:6

FATHER,

You are my Healer.

I thank You for doctors and medicine. I work with my doctors and do what needs to be done to help heal my body. But in the end, healing comes from You. You are the One who sends energy and strength back into my weak body. You are the One who heals all my diseases, physical and spiritual alike. I praise You for Your healing power and for the gift of restoration.

Amen.

The whole multitude sought to touch Him, for power went out from Him and healed them all.

LUKE 6:19

FATHER,

You want me to be whole.

There are no easy answers when it comes to healing, and there are so many things that I don't understand. But I do have confidence in the fact that You want me to be whole in my body and my soul and my spirit. On the days when I do not see the physical response I long for, I still trust Your intention for me. You want to heal me, and I trust the process, even when progress is slow. The power of healing comes from Your mighty hand.

Amen.

He said to him, "Do you want to be made well?"

JOHN 5:6

FATHER,

You reveal Your presence to me when I am facing illness.

Sometimes getting well is more difficult than being sick. As Your healing work begins in my body, I must begin to take responsibility for my life again. Being sick took me into a quiet place to be with You. Regaining my health means returning to a busy and distracting life. I am grateful that You are restoring me to health. Thank You for providing the hidden blessing in my illness—a time of deeper communion with You.

Amen.

•   •   •

When

I NEED HELP . . .

GOD *is our refuge and strength, A very present help in trouble.*

PSALM 46:1

FATHER,

You are here with me in my time of need.

I choose to place my trust in You. You are my safe Place, my Refuge from the storms of life. You are here with me now. I can rest safely in Your love, believing that You will act on my behalf. You make a way where there is no way. You are my Strength. I hold onto Your promises and claim them by faith. You do not leave me alone in my trouble—You rescue me.

Amen.

Lord, I believe; help my unbelief!

FATHER,

You strengthen my faith.

Even after all You have done for me, I still find myself doubting when I encounter troubles. I want to believe, but my fears rise up to challenge my faith. So I come to You now, asking that You help me in this time of crisis. My faith is small, but You are merciful. You strengthen me, give me promises to hold on to, and answer my prayers. Thank You that I can trust You to work on my behalf.

Amen.

> *Let us therefore come boldly to the throne of grace, that we may obtain mercy and find grace to help in time of need.*

HEBREWS 4:16

FATHER,

You tell me I can come to You boldly.

You fill my heart with faith and hope. You are my Helper, and You have mercy on me. I trust You with my whole heart. I know that You will send Your help to me at just the right time, in just the right way. Thank You for a bold faith that allows me to come before the throne of grace, knowing that Your love has made a safe way for me to find mercy in times of need. Thank You for giving me the privilege of coming to You.

Amen.

•   •   •

When

I NEED HOPE . . .

Now hope does not disappoint, because the love of God has been poured out in our hearts by the Holy Spirit who was given to us.

ROMANS 5:5

FATHER,

You do not disappoint me.

I dare to hope because I believe in You, and hoping in You is sure. Your ways are not my ways, and Your timing is often mysterious; but I have learned again and again that You can be trusted. So once again, I place my hope in You and trust You fully in my circumstance. You have poured Your love out on me, and I respond with hope and gratitude.

Amen.

Christ in you, the hope of glory.

COLOSSIANS 1:27

FATHER,

Your Son is my Door of hope.

I have hopes and dreams that cannot be fulfilled in this life. I have hope of seeing loved ones who have died and hope of a life without sorrow or suffering. It is Christ who raises from the dead, and it is Christ who is my Hope of glory in this life and in the next. When I am most inclined to despair, I meditate on the Incarnation of Your Son and thank You for the hope of eternal life.

Amen.

> *Hope in God; For I shall yet praise Him, The help of my countenance and my God.*

PSALM 42:11

FATHER,

You are my Hope.

I choose to place my hope in You. When my life is in chaos, when I am sad, and when hope seems far away; that is the time I most need to trust You. You will wipe away the tears from my eyes and restore my joy. My face will glow once again with gladness in Your love. My heart will be light because You have answered my prayers. Until the day of gladness, I continue to place my hope in You.

Amen.

> *Everyone who has this hope in Him purifies himself, just as He is pure.*

1 JOHN 3:3

FATHER,

You want what is best for me.

Lord, I know that sometimes I am the only one standing in the way of my well-being. You want to fulfill my best hopes. And that means I must become more of the person You called me to be and less of the self-centered person I used to be. I purify my heart because my hope is in You and not in my own ability to earn Your gift of grace.

Amen.

. . .

When

I AM JEALOUS . . .

Do not let your heart envy sinners, But in the fear of the LORD continue all day long.

FATHER,

You guard my heart tenderly.

I am ashamed that I should be so jealous of others. It is not so much that I envy what they have, but rather I envy what they represent—all the things I wish I could be and am not. In this situation I choose to take my eyes off the person who triggers feelings of jealousy. I choose instead to look to You. You see me as a beloved child created in Your own image. Help me see myself through Your eyes.

Amen.

110 • *Everyday Prayers for Everyday Cares*

He who glories, let him glory in the LORD.

1 CORINTHIANS 1:31

FATHER,

You deserve all glory.

Jealousy is a sign that I am worshipping something or someone other than You. Perhaps it is popularity or romance or power. Whatever it is, I have put people on pedestals, and now in my jealousy, I want to knock them off again. I ask You to cleanse my thoughts, renew my heart, and restore a right focus with You as the Center of my life. Then, I know that my heart will be clean before You.

Amen.

●   ●   ●

When

I NEED JOY . . .

Your word was to me the joy and rejoicing of my heart.

JEREMIAH 15:16

FATHER,

Your Word brings me joy.

You have given me precious promises in Your Word. Even more than that, You have given me stories of men and women of faith, psalms and songs that cover the entire spectrum of human emotion, and wise precepts that give me wisdom. Most of all, the story of Christ's life, death, and resurrection tells me how much You love all humankind. Your Word brings an ever-flowing fountain of joy in my heart.

Amen.

My soul shall be joyful in my God; For He
has clothed me with the garments of salvation.

FATHER,

You have clothed me with garments of salvation.

Even though I don't have much in this world, I am rich in the economy of the Kingdom of God. I am clothed in grace; I am a beloved child of the King of Kings. Because You have saved me, I am freed from my sin and able to enjoy life like a feast spread before me. I take joy in all You do and make my heart ready to receive the gifts You wish to lavish on me. I am joyous and free in Your love.

Amen.

Everyday Prayers for Everyday Cares • 113

"Until now you have asked nothing in My name. Ask, and you will receive, that your joy may be full."

JOHN 16:24

FATHER,

You give me a full measure of joy.

Thank you for the gift of joy. I celebrate the wonderful gifts You bring me and take joy in them. I thank You for the smell of morning coffee, the whisper of wind in the trees, a phone call from a friend, and the laughter of children. Before I even ask, You give me abundant blessings. I appreciate what I already have and only ask that You would continue to fill my heart with joy and gratitude for Your gifts.

Amen.

The kingdom of God is not eating and drinking, but righteousness and peace and joy in the Holy Spirit.

ROMANS 14:17

FATHER,

You are my Satisfaction.

The simple physical gift of daily bread comes in a myriad of forms: white, whole wheat, sourdough, rolls, muffins, crackers—the list is endless. Like the amazing variety of food and drink available to us, You also bring joy in many forms. Joy comes through people, places, things, and circumstances; yet all joy comes from one Source: You. I am thankful for the great variety of ways You bring righteousness, peace, and joy into my life.

Amen.

•   •   •

When

I Long to See Justice . . .

"He makes His sun rise on the evil and on the good, and sends rain on the just and on the unjust."

Matthew 5:45

FATHER,

You are an impartial and patient Judge.

You give me time and space to make my choices. You never coerce, threaten, or bully me. You are just, and You deal justly with Your children. Because Your plan is greater than I can imagine and Your ways are not my ways, I often wonder why You allow evil to have power over the good in this life. Nevertheless, I trust in You and Your infinite wisdom. In that I find my peace.

Amen.

> *Have you not shown partiality among your-*
> *selves, and become judges with evil thoughts¿*

JAMES 2:4

FATHER,

You show me my own heart.

It is so easy to judge others. Even when I think I am doing good, I often realize that I am showing partiality to those who are powerful, popular, influential, or wealthy. I have my own hidden opinions and prejudices. You show me the true state of my heart and cleanse me of my judgmental thoughts. You forgive me and help me to forgive others. You give me the gift of compassion, without which there is no true justice.

Amen.

He shall bring forth your righteousness as the light, And your justice as the noonday.

PSALM 37:6

FATHER,

You defend me from injustice.

In difficult times, when evil seems to rule and injustice seems to destroy the good, it is easy to forget that You are working in each situation. When I allow You to change my heart, it can be the beginning of greater change. One small decision can have many repercussions. Even when I do not see justice served right away, I choose to trust that You continue to defend the weak and the poor.

Amen.

> *Therefore, having been justified by faith, we have peace with God through our Lord Jesus Christ.*

ROMANS 5:1

FATHER,

You are merciful.

I have chosen to trust You for my justification, for I cannot justify myself. At this moment, I choose to rest in Your peace, knowing that You are the final Judge of all. You give the gift of faith to receive the grace that forgives, transforms, and saves. I can rest in Your tender mercies, which are new every morning. I am justified by faith, not by how hard I work. You are merciful to me.

Amen.

*   *   *

When

I FEEL LONELY . . .

"Greater love has no one than this, than to lay down one's life for his friends."

JOHN 15:13

FATHER,

Your Son laid down His life for me.

You loved the world so much that You sent Your only Son to us. And if I were the only one who needed to be saved, You still would have sent Jesus; and He still would have laid down His life for me. How can I be lonely when I have such a Friend? Lord, let my times of loneliness become gentle reminders of how much I am loved by You.

Amen.

> *"I will not leave you orphans; I will come to you."*

FATHER,

You will not forsake me.

I may feel alone in this world, but I am not. You are my Heavenly Father, and You love me. Your tender presence comforts me in every circumstance. I am your beloved child; so even if the world rejects me, I know I am accepted by You. You never leave me nor forsake me. I thank You for Your presence in my life and Your wonderful promises to me. You are the God who comforts the lonely.

Amen.

Casting all your care upon Him, for He cares for you.

1 PETER 5:7

FATHER,

You care for me.

When it seems that no one cares, I remember that You love me unconditionally and You care about what happens to me. But even more than that, You empower me to reach out to others. Because I have found love in You, that love overflows to others. You call me to be a friend to the friendless. You placed me in the family of God. When I bear another's burden, I can no longer be lonely.

Amen.

> *I will be glad and rejoice in Your mercy, For You have considered my trouble; You have known my soul in adversities.*

PSALM 31:7

FATHER,

You are always with me.

How grateful I am that You are happy to be with me! You know my soul intimately and walk with me in times of solitude. I discover gladness in our intimate communion. As we travel through life together, I realize that lonely times draw me closer to You and help me to understand myself better. When it is time to be with others again, I realize that my period of loneliness has taught me how to be a true friend.

Amen.

*   *   *

When

I LONG TO BE LOVED . . .

Behold what manner of love the Father has bestowed on us, that we should be called children of God!

1 JOHN 3:1

FATHER,

You love me.

Because You love me, I am learning what love is. And I am learning how to love You and others in return. Thank You for teaching me that love means reaching out to others and extending myself on their behalf. Thank You for showing me that love is about being patient, kind, and caring. It's about blessing others and putting their interests ahead of my own. Thank You for being a God of love and for shining the light of Your love on me. *Amen.*

My little children, let us not love in word or in tongue, but in deed and in truth.

1 JOHN 3:18

FATHER,

You teach me how to love others.

Because I learn lessons of love from You, I can better love others. You help me to be honest with myself, face my faults, and move beyond my own selfish needs. You show me simple ways to love others by offering a cup of cold water, a kind word, or simply a smile. You give me a compassionate awareness that others long for love just as much as my hungry heart yearns for it. How blessed it is to give to others that which I need the most: real love!

Amen.

To know the love of Christ which passes knowledge; that you may be filled with all the fullness of God.

FATHER,

You teach me how to love life.

Your creation fills my heart with wonder and amazement. Each day I find new mercies from Your hand. You teach me how to be aware of all the beauty and wonder life has to offer. You send simple daily gifts, and I have learned to be grateful for each one. You fill me with Your fullness, and I know that I am loved. Thank You for loving me and teaching me how to love the life You have given me.

Amen.

Let brotherly love continue.

FATHER,

You send people to show me Your love.

When I am going through a tough time, my pride often keeps me from reaching out to others. Yet it seems that just when I feel that way, You send someone along who is supportive and caring—just what I really need. Thank You for extending Your care through people in my life. And thank You for loving me even more than I love myself.

Amen.

•   •   •

When

I NEED HELP IN MY MARRIAGE . . .

Let the husband render to his wife the affection due her, and likewise also the wife to her husband.

1 CORINTHIANS 7:3

FATHER,

You teach me to love in practical ways.

Today I choose to find ways to meet the needs of my spouse without expecting anything in return. Simple gestures of affection—kind words, a gentle touch, and helpful acts—are the small seeds that will one day reap a harvest of blessings that come from a strengthened marriage. I give all my expectations and worries to You. Give me the energy to love my mate in practical ways that demonstrate genuine affection.

Amen.

Hatred stirs up strife, But love covers all sins.

PROVERBS 10:12

FATHER,

You help me to see my mate with loving eyes.

My spouse and I know each other so well that we finish each other's sentences and anticipate each other's actions. But even though we know one another so intimately, I still find that the person I married is a mystery to me. Lord, let me look at my spouse with new eyes. Let me appreciate the mystery of this changing human being who shares my home and my life. Let me look past skin-deep problems and see the heart within.

Amen.

• • •

When

I NEED MERCY . . .

Through the LORD's mercies we are not consumed, Because His compassions fail not. They are new every morning. Great is Your faithfulness.

LAMENTATIONS 3:22-23

FATHER,

Your mercies are new every morning.

You surround me with love, compassion, and kindness. You are always faithful, ever near. When I cry out for help, You answer. You save me from my sin. You give me strength in my weakness. Every morning when I wake, I take a moment to praise You for the gift of life. Even on the most difficult days, You give me strength to stand strong. Weeping may endure for a night, but I know joy comes in the morning.

Amen.

> *"Blessed are the merciful, For they shall obtain mercy."*

MATTHEW 5:7

FATHER,

You are merciful.

By showing mercy, I receive mercy in return. Because You show compassion to me in my weakness, I can show compassion to others when they are feeling weak. I do not need to judge others because I do not need to justify myself. When I am compassionate, compassion is given to me. Thank You that Your mercy extends to all and Your kindness is never exhausted.

Amen.

•   •   •

When

I NEED PATIENCE . . .

The testing of your faith produces patience.

JAMES 1:3

FATHER,

You teach me patience.

As I walk through this difficult time, I am learning to be patient. With Your help, I am becoming less anxious in my waiting. You are patient and persistent with me, and You teach me how to incorporate those qualities into my life. You want only the best for me—and the best takes time. You develop the qualities in me that enable me to live life fully and completely.

Amen.

See how the farmer waits for the precious fruit of the earth, waiting patiently for it until it receives the early and latter rain.

FATHER,

You show me the fruit of patience.

In our society, we expect instant results. We take short cuts, and we measure productivity by quantity of work rather than quality. But in Your Kingdom, a different kind of economy is at work. Like a golden field of wheat or a tree-lined orchard, fruitfulness comes slowly over time. And You teach me the benefits of such patience. Then, instead of a forced, assembly-line existence, I am able to enjoy an abundant and fruitful life.

Amen.

I WAITED patiently for the LORD; And He inclined to me, And heard my cry.

PSALM 40:1

FATHER,

I wait patiently for You.

You are worth waiting for. You do not come to me on my schedule, but instead You come when the time is right. You see down the road and know what lies ahead. If I patiently wait for You, things work out for the best. All my worry and hurry cannot make an apple ripen faster. Nor will my fretting make things come together any sooner in my life. So I stop worrying. I look to You and listen to Your voice. I rest in You, waiting patiently for Your perfect timing.

Amen.

> *"The ones that fell on the good ground are those who, having heard the word with a noble and good heart, keep it and bear fruit with patience."*

LUKE 8:15

FATHER,

I quietly trust You.

Like an expectant mother waiting for the time when her baby will be born, I wait quietly while You work on my behalf. I live expectantly, secure in the knowledge that my times are in Your hands. Growth comes in increments, and good things take time. You have good things planned for me, and I wait patiently in Your presence for You to bring them to pass.

Amen.

•   •   •

When

I NEED PEACE . . .

"Peace I leave with you, My peace I give to you; not as the world gives do I give to you."

JOHN 14:27

FATHER,

You give me peace.

The world can be a violent place. Death and destruction are in our daily headlines. We arm ourselves with burglar alarms to keep thieves from breaking in and with armies to keep war from breaking out. But You do not need bombs and bayonets, soldiers and laws. For You bring peace to the heart—a peace that passes all understanding. When I long for peace in a weary world, I look to You.

Amen.

> *You will keep him in perfect peace, Whose mind is stayed on You, Because he trusts in You.*

ISAIAH 26:3

FATHER,

I find peace in You.

I can be a champion worrier. I can fret over any problem, large or small. It's easy to concentrate on the problem. But Lord, You are the Solution to every situation. You are the One who protects, guides, and saves me. So I turn my attention to who You are: You are faithful and trustworthy. I allow Your Spirit to bring peace to my heart, and I still my busy mind by meditating on Your faithfulness.

Amen.

> *You shall go out with joy, And be led out with peace; The mountains and the hills Shall break forth into singing before you, And all the trees of the field shall clap their hands.*

ISAIAH 55:12

FATHER,

I find peace in Your creation.

One day there will be a final peace and a complete joy. All the earth will be redeemed. But until that time, Your beautiful creation offers a small picture of that coming day. New green leaves in spring, a blossoming rose in summer, a golden twilight in autumn, the frozen stillness of a pond in winter—all remind me of the peace that comes only from You.

Amen.

> *Now may the God of hope fill you with all joy*
> *and peace in believing, that you may abound*
> *in hope by the power of the Holy Spirit.*

ROMANS 15:13

FATHER,

You fill me with the gifts of peace and joy.

And those gifts make room for more and more of Your blessings, such as hope and faith. When my heart is disturbed and fretful, I will choose peace, knowing that all Your wonderful gifts will follow. Thank You for giving me exactly what I need for each day. Thank You for opening my heart to see Your goodness to me in the midst of turmoil.

Amen.

•   •   •

When

I Am Prideful . . .

"Therefore whoever humbles himself as this little child is the greatest in the kingdom of heaven."

MATTHEW 18:4

FATHER,

You value the simplicity of a child's heart.

Oftentimes, I want others to think that I am a smart, sophisticated, and confident person. But every time I try to play those games, I get hurt, and my pride is trampled on. I need to remember that the real me, the one who lives deep inside my heart, is not a sophisticated person. I am simply a child. I am Your child. And today I enjoy the privileges of being in that position—a humble child loved by my Father.

Amen.

"When you are invited by anyone to a wedding feast, do not sit down in the best place."

LUKE 14:8

FATHER,

You teach me humility.

This world tells me that I must push my way to the top, get what I need before someone else takes it, and remind others that they are not better than I am. But when I follow that advice, I am being prideful and am ignoring Your wisdom. I don't want to live that way anymore. Today I choose a different path. I will let my work speak for itself, instead of bragging about it. I will trust You to provide for me. I will honor others above myself. Thank You for teaching me a better way.

Amen.

•　•　•

When

I NEED HELP WITH PRIORITIES . . .

"Seek first the kingdom of God and His righteousness, and all these things shall be added to you."

MATTHEW 6:33

FATHER,

You want me to seek You above all else.

Help me to give Your will first place in my life. As I look at what I need to accomplish this day, this week, and this month, I choose to honor the vision and purpose You have placed in my life. And I choose to do those things that are pleasing to You—to be honest in my dealings, to speak the truth no matter what it costs, and to freely forgive those who trespass against me. Thank You for making Your will alive in my heart.

Amen.

> *The fear of the LORD is the beginning of knowl-
> edge, But fools despise wisdom and instruction.*

PROVERBS 1:7

FATHER,

You instruct me in the way I should go.

I have organized my "to do" lists, my flow charts, and my daily schedules. These plans are my best guesses at what will happen in my life. But I cannot anticipate all the possibilities or plan for all the contingencies. So I depend on Your wisdom and guidance each day. I will do the best I can and then trust that You will lead and instruct me. I take time to listen and learn from You.

Amen.

A word fitly spoken is like apples of gold in settings of silver.

PROVERBS 25:11

FATHER,

You help me to speak wisely.

Sometimes I let my mouth run ahead of my brain. But You teach me to listen to my heart and to speak with compassion and wisdom. Instead of pretending to listen to others, I concentrate on really hearing what is being said. I listen for what is unspoken as well as what is spoken. I keep my eyes open and am aware of hidden undercurrents in situations. Thank You for helping me to make other people a priority in my life.

Amen.

> *Do not boast about tomorrow, For you do not know what a day may bring forth.*

PROVERBS 27:1

FATHER,

You know all of my days.

Each day begins with Your mercy and ends with Your grace. You help me decide what is important and necessary as well as what can be eliminated from my "to do" list. When unexpected situations come up, You guide me. When opportunity arises, You help me make the most of it. As each day unfolds, I listen to Your voice of wisdom that instructs and encourages me. You help me keep my priorities straight.

Amen.

•   •   •

When

I NEED PROTECTION . . .

---

*He shall cover you with His feathers, And
under His wings you shall take refuge.*

PSALM 91:4

FATHER,

You are my Protector.

When I am in the midst of danger and difficulty, You
are always with me. You are constantly guiding me,
reminding me to use common sense and intuition.
Sometimes, You send people into my life to bring me a
word of wisdom and caution. But somehow You always
provide the help I need to avoid disastrous circumstances
and to keep my feet on the safe path. You are a present
Help in trouble.

Amen.

> *The fear of man brings a snare, But whoever trusts in the LORD shall be safe.*

PROVERBS 29:25

FATHER,

You are the One I trust.

Danger does not only lurk in dark alleys. It can also come in the midst of a quiet conversation. I can allow myself to feel angry or intimidated, or I can rest in You. When someone intends to harm me, I am safest when I make You my Refuge. You protect me from those who intimidate and misuse their power. You show me a way out of danger to a safe place.

Amen.

•   •   •

When

I NEED HELP WITH MY RELATIONSHIPS . . .

He who does not love does not know God, for God is love.

---

1 JOHN 4:8

FATHER,

You help me to love.

My relationships with others reflect my relationship with You. You are Love. You deal with me gently, mercifully, and kindly. When I am unkind, judgmental, and harsh, I am not acting like Your child. When I forgive others, encourage others, and appreciate their individuality, I am reflecting to others the way I have been treated by You. When others look at me, I pray that they can see Your love in my eyes.

Amen.

Like a flitting sparrow, like a flying swallow,
So a curse without cause shall not alight.

PROVERBS 26:2

FATHER,

You teach me to be careful what I say.

It is too easy to let my tongue slip. A little gossip here, a snide comment there—suddenly I find myself in the quicksand that drowns my relationships. Help me to be compassionate to others. Help me to speak kindly and not to spread gossip. When I am angry, help me to keep my mouth shut. Please keep me from sins of presumption, so that my harsh words do not boomerang back on me.

Amen.

Go from the presence of a foolish man,
When you do not perceive in him the lips of
knowledge.

PROVERBS 14:7

FATHER,

You give me discernment.

Sometimes I can be swept away by charm and good looks. It's easy to get caught up in the excitement of a strong personality. But You teach me to look beneath the surface charm. I ask the questions, "Does this person have a good heart? Do I trust this person? Am I allowing flattery to carry me away? What is the true worth of this relationship?" Thank You for helping me to be discerning about whom I trust.

Amen.

> *"Therefore, whatever you want men to do to you, do also to them, for this is the Law and the Prophets."*

MATTHEW 7:12

FATHER,

You remind me of the golden rule.

"Do unto others before they do unto you" is the slogan for a competitive market economy—or so we are often told. But I want to live by Your standards for growth. I treat others as I wish to be treated. I turn the other cheek whenever possible. I maintain long-term relationships and seek to do good to each person I meet. You help me relate to others from a pure heart when I live by the golden rule.

Amen.

•   •   •

I NEED RESTORATION . . .

He leads me beside the still waters. He restores my soul.

PSALMS 23:2-3

FATHER,

You restore my soul.

When I am frazzled by a hectic day or tired from dealing with a difficult situation, I find restoration in You. I close the door on the noisy world, come to You with my problems, and quiet my spirit in Your presence. My soul finds restoration in time alone with You. Whether it is a few minutes in the midst of the day or a devotional time in the evening, You meet me and restore my soul.

Amen.

I have seen his ways, and will heal him; I will also lead him, And restore comforts to him.

ISAIAH 57:18

FATHER,

You help me find rest.

Sometimes the best thing to do is to take a break. When life is tearing me down, I have learned to retreat and rest for a while. Because I trust in You, I can give myself permission to stop, to get away, and to regain my perspective. You have taught me to take small vacations—to stop and smell the roses. I play with a pet, work in the garden, go for a walk, or go see a movie. Thank You for teaching me to find restoration through rest.

Amen.

* * *

When

I FEEL SHAME . . .

---

*Create in me a clean heart, O God, And
renew a steadfast spirit within me.*

PSALM 51:10

FATHER,

You give me a clean heart.

The hidden sins that darken my heart are painful to
You. But when I confess them, You forgive. Your grace
gives me a clean heart. When my heart is clean, I am sure
of Your love. Because You love me, I am able to discern
where my feelings of shame come from. If the shame is
deserved, You forgive me. If the shame is undeserved,
You renew my spirit and help me continue to grow in
Your grace.

Amen.

There is therefore now no condemnation to those who are in Christ Jesus, who do not walk according to the flesh, but according to the Spirit.

FATHER,

You do not condemn me.

It seems like so often I come to You, ashamed of my actions, asking once again for Your forgiveness. How grateful I am that You do not condemn me, but, instead, lift me up and help me find new perspective! If I need to make apologies or restoration, You show me the best way to do so. If there is nothing more I can do to repair the situation, You give me peace. Thank you for Your grace in my life.

Amen.

•   •   •

When

I NEED STABILITY . . .

Cast your burden on the LORD, And He shall sustain you; He shall never permit the righteous to be moved.

PSALM 55:22

FATHER,

You establish me in Your love.

In times of trouble and chaos, I depend on You. You quiet my fears and speak peace to the emotional storms that rage in my heart. I steady myself by meditating on Your faithfulness. You are my strong Foundation, the One who helps me keep my balance in the midst of the storm. I thank You for sustaining me in the way that I should go and helping me to stand strong even in the midst of adverse circumstances.

Amen.

> *A man is not established by wickedness, But the root of the righteous cannot be moved.*

PROVERBS 12:3

FATHER,

You help me to be grounded in You.

In the midst of change and confusion, You are my Foundation. Because You are with me, steadying my footsteps, I am like a tree planted by streams of living water. My leaf never withers. Storm or drought, rain or shine, the weather on the outside cannot move me because I place my trust in You. Circumstances may change, but You are always the same. I am rooted and grounded in You.

Amen.

* * *

When

I NEED STRENGTH . . .

"My grace is sufficient for you, for My strength is made perfect in weakness."

2 CORINTHIANS 12:9

FATHER,

You are my Strength.

When I am feeling weak or helpless, You are with me. I can lean on You and trust You to provide all I need. Thank You for not despising me for my weakness but for using it instead to bring strength and stability to my life. I will always praise You for working through my weakness to accomplish Your purpose in every situation I am facing.

Amen.

> *Those who wait on the LORD Shall renew their strength.*

ISAIAH 40:31

FATHER,

You renew my strength.

Thank You for teaching me that my strength is not a matter of pushing myself until I drop. But rather, it comes from respecting my need for rest and renewal. I rest my mind by turning my worries over to You. I rest my spirit by letting You cradle my heart tenderly. I take the time to be quiet and wait on You, and my strength is renewed.

Amen.

> *I will love You, O LORD, my strength. The LORD is my rock and my fortress and my deliverer.*

FATHER,

You help me find my own strength.

Thank You for helping me to develop my faith. As athletes gradually strengthen their muscles or artists slowly build their skills, I, too, am daily building my own spiritual strength. I study Your Word, take time to pray, go to worship regularly, and develop my spiritual life. You strengthen me in Your love. You are my Strength when I need it.

Amen.

Now to Him who is able to do exceedingly abundantly above all that we ask or think, according to the power that works in us.

FATHER,

You give me abundant strength.

When I ask for strength, You give me more than I could ever ask or think. Your power is great. You are the Creator of the earth, the Mighty One who delivered Israel, and the Savior of the world. You are the God of abundant strength, with more than enough to meet my needs. I praise You that Your hand holds me, that Your will is perfect, and that You are powerful and strong to works on my behalf.

Amen.

•　　•　　•

When

I FEEL STRESSED . . .

Then they cried out to the LORD in their trouble,
And He saved them out of their distresses.

PSALM 107:19

FATHER,

You save me from my distress.

Sometimes I fill my schedule too full and add too many burdens to my life because I am trying too hard to please others. I rush through my life and lose the joy of living. Today I choose to make simple changes in my life—changes that will help me find the quietness and peace I so desperately need. Thank You for delivering me from my stressful lifestyle and for helping me make the choices that lead to peace and wholeness.

Amen.

Let the peace of God rule in your hearts.

COLOSSIANS 3:15

FATHER,

You calm my heart.

I have let the pace of my "hurry-up" society rule my life. Now it is time to let You set the pace of my life again. Instead of living by the clock, I choose to live in a more eternal rhythm. I will meet my obligations, but I will not pile obligation upon obligation. Thank You for calming my heart in the midst of my busy day. You keep me in touch with the timing of Heaven. I'm so grateful that You are Ruler over the entire earth—and over me.

Amen.

Be still, and know that I am God.

PSALM 46:10

FATHER,

You still my anxious spirit.

Thank You for showing me that I need to take time away from the rush and noise of modern life. You help me to stay healthy by calling me to times of rest and quiet. I turn off the TV and close the door on all distractions. I circle a date with You on my calendar. I read Your Word and meditate on Your promises. I sit in Your presence and worship. You quiet my soul as a mother quiets her child.

Amen.

> *Better is a little with the fear of the LORD,*
> *Than great treasure with trouble.*

PROVERBS 15:16

FATHER,

You are all I need.

I don't need to be a millionaire to find satisfaction in life. I don't need to add extra stress to my life trying to keep up with my neighbors. I can be happy with the gifts You give me. I can enjoy the simple pleasures that make my life worthwhile. I can say no to overloading my schedule so that I will have time to enjoy being Your child. You satisfy my heart, and I find rest and peace in You.

Amen.

•   •   •

When

I LONG TO SUCCEED . . .

Keep your heart with all diligence, For out of it spring the issues of life.

PROVERBS 4:23

FATHER,

You motivate me.

When I find myself wondering if I will ever reach my goals, You strengthen my heart and reinforce my resolve. You reveal my motives to me and help me keep them pure. You teach me to value true success and discern between what is real and what is false. Thank You for keeping my feet on the right path and making it possible for me to fulfill my dreams.

Amen.

The Lord is my fort where I can enter and be safe; no one can follow me in and slay me.

PSALM 18:2 TLB

FATHER,

You help me choose good companions.

Thank You for the friends You have given me. Without their encouragement and wisdom, I don't know how I would reach my goals. You have sent just the right people to keep me healthy and strong—those who will tell me the truth when I need to hear it. In the same way, You help me to see through the shallow devices of those with deceitful motives. I am blessed because You are directing me.

Amen.

The testimony of the LORD is sure, making wise the simple.

PSALM 19:7

FATHER,

You give me the tools for success.

There are plenty of people who would like to teach me how to succeed—for a price. But You, Lord, are the best Teacher because You begin by teaching me how to be a successful human being. You help me build character and recognize character in others. You guide me to the right people, the right ideas, the right tools, and the right solutions for creating true success. You are all I need.

Amen.

*Establish the work of our hands for us; Yes,
establish the work of our hands.*

PSALM 90:17

FATHER,

You bless the work that I do.

Thank You for blessing the work I do and for teaching
me to be conscientious and careful. Thank You for inspir-
ing me to create good things that are useful and beautiful. Because of You, I can be proud of the work I produce.
You bless my hands, my heart, and my mind, making me
so much better than I really am. My work is successful
because You have blessed it.

Amen.

•   •   •

When

I DON'T UNDERSTAND SUFFERING . . .

I will ascribe justice to my Maker. Be assured that my words are not false; one perfect in knowledge is with you.

JOB 36:3-4 NIV

FATHER,

You are merciful and just.

I do not understand when people suffer unjustly. It hurts me to see needless pain. The starving child in a famine-struck land looks at me with big sorrowful eyes. A plane crashes, and people die. An evil ruler steals from his country's citizens. Though I do not understand how these things can be, I know that You are good and merciful. Thank You for comforting my heart in the midst of this world's sorrow.

Amen.

"Blessed are those who mourn, For they shall be comforted."

MATTHEW 5:4

FATHER,

You comfort me when I mourn.

When suffering is too much to bear, I come to You. I shed tears of sorrow in Your presence. I bring my burdens to You. Though I have no answers and no easy solutions, I find comfort in Your love. I move beyond my questions into a communion with You because You have also experienced suffering. No matter what I must endure, I find my comfort in You and Your love for me.

Amen.

• • •

When

I STRUGGLE WITH
TEMPTATION . . .

---

*No temptation has overtaken you except such
as is common to man; but God is faithful.*

1 CORINTHIANS 10:13

FATHER,

You are faithful when I am tempted.

Temptation calls to me. It tells me that I need to take a shortcut to happiness. It says that there is an easy way and this is it. But You help me resist temptation. You are my Strength when I am weak. You are my strong Tower in the midst of a flood of evil. You are there to hold my hand, to lead me away from temptation, and to help me find faith in You once more.

Amen.

> *Blessed is the man who endures temptation;*
> *for when he has been approved, he will*
> *receive the crown of life which the Lord has*
> *promised to those who love Him.*

JAMES 1:12

FATHER,

You help me endure.

Sometimes I let anger and resentment make me weak and vulnerable to temptation. But when I turn to You, my strength is renewed. You help me to lay aside those things that threaten to weigh me down and debase me. And You show that forgiveness and reconciliation is a better way. Because of You, I have the courage to overcome temptation and keep my heart pleasing to You.

Amen.

• • •

When

I AM THANKFUL . . .

Rejoice always, pray without ceasing, in everything give thanks.

1 THESSALONIANS 5:16-18

FATHER,

You deserve my boundless gratitude.

How good You are to me! How wonderful is Your love and kindness! I rejoice in all the blessings and good gifts You have given me and will continue to give me in the future. You are my Provider, and You watch over me with great love. I can never thank You enough for this gift of life. My heart overflows with gratitude, and I praise You for Your never-ending kindness.

Amen.

> *Enter into His gates with thanksgiving, And into His courts with praise. Be thankful to Him, and bless His name.*

PSALM 100:4

FATHER,

You are the Lord of Life.

You are the God who gives me life. From my first breath to my last, You surround me with blessings. Though I came to You with nothing, You have given me all I need and more. And You not only meet my needs, but You also expand my heart so that I can receive even more from You—more love, more peace, and more joy.

Amen.

Giving thanks always for all things.

Ephesians 5:20

FATHER,

You inspire praise in all circumstances.

I thank You for being with me in every situation, especially the difficult ones. You have always proven yourself faithful, no matter what situation I've faced. I thank You for deliverance, healing, and resolution. I also thank You for the mysteries and unanswered questions of life. You know all things, and You hold all mysteries in Your hands. I can trust You when life is difficult, believing You work all things together for good.

Amen.

Oh, give thanks to the LORD, for He is good!
For His mercy endures forever.

PSALM 136:1

FATHER,

Your mercy and grace surround me.

You are so patient and loving with me. I thank You for Your grace and mercy. You do not condemn or treat me harshly. Instead, You are a loving Father who will never leave me nor forsake me. I see Your blessings in so many small ways. And I am especially grateful for the daily tender mercies You extend to me. Thank You for enriching my life with Your grace.

Amen.

•   •   •

When

I AM FACING A TRAGEDY . . .

Unto the upright there arises light in the darkness; He is gracious, and full of compassion, and righteous.

PSALM 112:4

FATHER,

You are there in the darkest night.

When my heart reaches out for answers and explanations and finds none, I'm so grateful that You are there, drawing me close in the midst of my night. Your comfort helps me to make it through until the light of dawn arrives. You are my Strength and steadying Arm until the sun rises again over the landscape of my life. When I face tragedy, I will trust in You for You are full of mercy.

Amen.

> *God will wipe away every tear from their eyes; there shall be no more death, nor sorrow, nor crying. There shall be no more pain, for the former things have passed away.*

REVELATION 21:4

FATHER,

You are my eternal Healer.

Even now, I am facing a sorrow so deep, a loss so overwhelming that I would despair of life if it were not for Your presence. You embrace me and keep me from freezing during my cold night of grief. You remind me that You are the Resurrection and the Life. You breathe renewed hope into my devastated heart. You give me the strength to go on with my life, knowing that You will never leave me.

Amen.

* * *

When

I WANT TO KNOW TRUTH . . .

> *"You shall know the truth, and the truth shall make you free."*

JOHN 8:32

FATHER,

Your truth sets me free.

Sometimes I avoid the truth, longing for easy answers and simple lies. I'm tempted to listen to flattering tongues that tell me what I want to hear. But You are faithful to overcome my destructive behaviors and call me to truth and repentance. You urge me to follow the right path, even when it is a difficult one. You make me face my fears and disarm them. And as I face the truth, You set me free.

Amen.

Behold, You desire truth in the inward parts,
And in the hidden part You will make me to
know wisdom.

PSALM 51:6

FATHER,

You call me to live in truth.

You know me. I may be able to fool others, but I cannot fool You. You know my shortcomings, my sins, my half-truths, and my evasions. You are merciful and forgiving. But You are also a just God. You will not leave me in my sins or encourage my bad habits. You challenge me to follow You from my deepest heart. You show me that the way of truth is the way to life everlasting.

Amen.

*   *   *

When

I NEED WISDOM . . .

Wisdom is better than rubies, And all the things one may desire cannot be compared with her.

PROVERBS 8:11

FATHER,

Your wisdom is my greatest treasure.

I know, Lord, that I might have a bounty of money, cars, homes, and all the best of earthly possessions; but unless I have wisdom, they are no good to me at all. Therefore, I long for what only You can give—wisdom that will be with me throughout this life and into the next. Thank You for the wisdom You bring to me and the peace and stability that wisdom creates in the midst of my daily circumstances.

Amen.

Turn away my eyes from looking at worthless things, And revive me in Your way.

PSALM 119:37

FATHER,

You help me to focus on what is important.

Constant distractions fill my day, crying for attention and drawing me away from those things that are truly meaningful in my life. Thank You for providing the wisdom I need to live my life in a way that is pleasing to You. Without Your help, I would be helpless to sort through the clamor and find the proper course for my day. Thank You for keeping my feet on the right path.

Amen.

Your word is a lamp to my feet And a light to my path.

PSALM 119:105

FATHER,

You give me wisdom.

When I need wisdom most, You provide it for me in the pages of the Bible. As I read, You open my heart and mind to see solutions to my problems and principles for enriching my daily life. Thank You for giving me Your Word to guide and direct me through all the twists and turns my path will take and for promising to bring me safely to my destination.

Amen.

> *Wisdom is the principal thing; Therefore get wisdom. And in all your getting, get understanding.*

PROVERBS 4:7

FATHER,

Your extend Your greatest treasures to me.

Your wisdom is greater than I can fathom—and You want to share that wisdom with me. I share in the riches of Your understanding, constantly growing in grace and learning how great Your love is for me. You offer insight and wisdom to those who seek You. You give me understanding that lights my way in this life. You have given me many gifts, but wisdom is a gift that teaches me how to truly live.

Amen.

*   *   *

When

I NEED HELP IN
MY WORK . . .

---

*The generous soul will be made rich, And he
who waters will also be watered himself.*

PROVERBS 11:25

FATHER,

You call me to lift up others.

My human nature calls me to be a star, standing head
and shoulders above my co-workers, grabbing up the
credit, and ensuring my place in the spotlight. But You
urge me down a different path—a path that leads to
cooperation and team work. You have shown me that
anger, jealousy, and pride will steal the joy and excellence
from my work. I humble myself before You, Lord. Teach
me to love and lift up others.

Amen.

> *"Well done, good and faithful servant; you have been faithful over a few things, I will make you ruler over many things."*

MATTHEW 25:23

FATHER,

You are honored by work faithfully done.

So often I am tempted to withhold my best, doing only what is required. But as I submit my work to You, I am learning a better way. I am learning that when I give less than my all, I do not honor You with my work. I want You to know that I'm grateful for the gifts and abilities You have placed in my life. Help me always to please You by doing my work as well as I possibly can.

Amen.

> *Doing the will of God from the heart, with good will doing service, as to the Lord, and not to men.*

EPHESIANS 6:6-7

FATHER,

You are the Reason I work faithfully.

When I am tired and discouraged, tempted to give less than my best, I remember Your love for me and the great blessings You have placed in my life. Your love motivates me to do the right thing and to reach out to You for the strength I need to do it. You gave me not only gifts and abilities, but also the determination to use them to their fullest.

Amen.

> *Be diligent to know the state of your flocks,*
> *And attend to your herds.*

PROVERBS 27:23

FATHER,

You help me develop my skills.

Though I do not herd sheep and goats like the psalmist of old, I do need to attend to my work. As Michelangelo knew the marble, Beethoven his instrument, and Shakespeare his language, so I also must intimately know the work I have before me. I look to You to help me remain faithful as I develop the gifts and talents You have placed in my life. Show me, Lord, how to use each one for Your glory.

Amen.

•   •   •

> *Search me, O God, and know my heart; Try*
> *me, and know my anxieties; And see if there*
> *is any wicked way in me, And lead me in the*
> *way everlasting.*

PSALMS 139:23-24

FATHER,

You calm my anxieties.

It is easy to worry. I can think of a dozen things to worry about right this minute. I ask that You search my heart and reveal my true motives so I can be honest with You. Thank You for helping me to put my worries aside and turn to look at You in faith. You calm my fears. You know my anxieties. You lead me in the way of life—a life of faith in which there is no room for fear.

Amen.

> *The fear of the LORD leads to life, And he who has it will abide in satisfaction; He will not be visited with evil.*

PROVERBS 19:23

FATHER,

You lead me to life.

When I am worried, I come to You, for You are the One who can put my fears to flight and provide the strength I need to choose life. You are the One whose faithfulness gives me the courage to find creative solutions for my problems rather than rehearsing them over and over in my mind. I know that You have never failed me, and I continue to place my trust in You.

Amen.

• • •

Additional copies of this book and other
titles from Honor Books
are available from your local bookstore.

Everyday Prayers for Everyday Cares for Women
Everyday Prayers for Everyday Cares for Mothers
Everyday Prayers for Everyday Cares for Parents

If you have enjoyed this book,
or if it has impacted your life,
we would like to hear from you.

Please contact us at:

Honor Books
Department E
P.O. Box 55388
Tulsa, Oklahoma 74155
Or by e-mail at *info@honorbooks.com*